CW01209272

A-Z
of
ENDANGERED ANIMALS

ALSO BY JENNIFER COSSINS

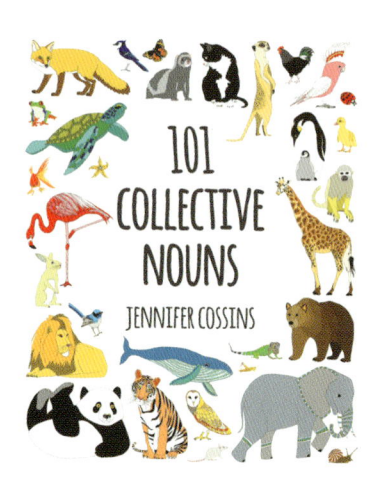

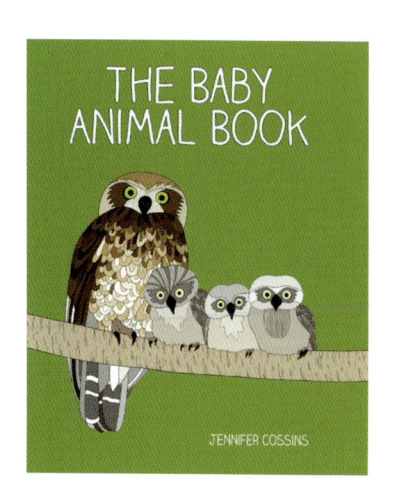

A-Z
OF
ENDANGERED ANIMALS

JENNIFER COSSINS

LOTHIAN
Children's Books

A Lothian Children's Book

This edition published in Australia and New Zealand in 2017
by Hachette Australia
Level 17, 207 Kent Street, Sydney NSW 2000
www.hachettechildrens.com.au

First published in Australia and New Zealand in 2016
by Red Parka Press

3 5 7 9 10 8 6 4 2

Text and illustration copyright © Jennifer Cossins 2016

This book is copyright. Apart from any fair dealing for the purposes of private study, research, criticism or review permitted under the *Copyright Act 1968*, no part may be stored or reproduced by any process without prior written permission. Enquiries should be made to the publisher.

Cataloguing-in-Publication data available
from the National Library of Australia

ISBN 978 0 7344 1795 4 (hardback)
ISBN 978 0 7344 1857 9 (paperback)

Designed by Red Parka Press
Printed in China by Toppan Leefung Printing Limited

THIS BOOK IS DEDICATED
TO TRACY AND TESS.
MY A TO Z.

CONTENTS

A – AMUR TIGER
B – BLUE WHALE
C – CRESTED PENGUIN
D – DUGONG
E – EASTERN GORILLA
F – FIJIAN IGUANA
G – GIANT PANDA
H – HELMETED HORNBILL
I – INDIAN ELEPHANT
J – JOCOTOCO ANTPITTA
K – KAKAPO
L – LEATHERBACK TURTLE
M – MANDRILL

N – NUMBAT
O – ORANGUTAN
P – PYGMY THREE-TOED SLOTH
Q – QUOKKA
R – RED PANDA
S – SNOW LEOPARD
T – TASMANIAN DEVIL
U – UMBRELLABIRD
V – VAQUITA
W – WHALE SHARK
X – XINJIANG GROUND JAY
Y – YELLOW CARDINAL
Z – ZEBRA DUIKER

INTRODUCTION

Our planet is home to well over seven million different animal species. Everywhere you look there is life, even in the driest desert, the deepest ocean and the coldest peak of the highest mountain. Life on this beautiful planet we call Earth is truly remarkable!

Sadly, we are currently in the midst of a wave of mass extinction unlike anything since the demise of the dinosaurs. Extinctions of the past were driven by natural disasters (events like the Ice Age) and as a natural part of evolution. However, the current extinction rate is more than 100 times higher than the historical rate and it is being driven by the success of one singular species: humans. During the last 500 years, over 800 species have become extinct and over 10,000 more are considered threatened. This is based on available data, true numbers may well be much higher.

The most common reason for extinction today is habitat loss. As the human population grows, many animals have been forced into smaller areas. Ecosystems such as forests, grasslands and deserts have been cleared or damaged to allow for crop planting, cattle grazing and development of roads, housing and factories. Humans are also responsible for pollution as well as contributing to climate change – two factors that drastically impact animals by further degrading their habitats.

Another major threat to our endangered animals is introduced species. Ever since humans began crossing the oceans, animals such as cats, weasels, rats, rabbits and foxes have found their way to foreign lands and have wreaked havoc on native animals. In Australia, rabbits and foxes are driving many native marsupials to extinction, whereas in New Zealand, the weasel has almost succeeded in wiping out the flightless kakapo.

Contributing further to the current wave of extinction is exploitation, such as hunting, collecting or trading animals. Animals have always been hunted by humans but early humans lived in harmony with nature, killing animals only for essentials like food and clothing. Today, animals are killed for meat, clothing, feathers, ivory, eggs, medicines, hunting trophies, tourism and even entertainment. Many species are still highly prized in the illegal exotic pet trade.

This all paints a dark picture. However, there are many individuals and organisations around the world dedicated to protecting our endangered animals and, while it's too late for some, there is much we can do to help save those we have left. Large international organisations like the World Wildlife Fund and Greenpeace, numerous regional groups such as Animals Australia, as well as countless local organisations are working towards better protection of our animals and environment. Governments and corporate groups have helped in some areas too, with around 10% of the planet designated as protected areas over the last century. Marine reserves only account for 1% of the oceans, and although we have come a long way both on land and at sea, so much more needs to be done to save many of our threatened species.

I believe it is our responsibility as humans to protect animals from extinction. In doing so, we also protect our planet's biodiversity, which is essential to our own survival, longevity and happiness as a species as well as that of the animals described in this book.

The tragic reality is that more species become threatened every day and they will become extinct if we do not act quickly to save them. But please do not despair! Each and every one of us can help by doing small things every day, like keeping our beaches clean, reusing and recycling household items and not wasting water. We can also learn more about the plight of animals, petition our governments to do more to help, and support the organisations out there on the frontline fighting to save endangered animals.

I hope you enjoy exploring and learning about the unique, fragile and very special animals in this book and that you will feel inspired to take action yourself to help save them. Our planet and future generations need us!

A IS FOR...

CONSERVATION STATUS: ENDANGERED	POPULATION: AROUND 540

The Amur tiger, also known as the Siberian tiger, is the largest cat in the world. They can be over 4 metres long (including the tail) and weigh up to 320 kilograms. Amur tigers differ from other tigers because they have fewer, paler stripes and they also have manes.

The Amur tiger is found in small pockets of the Russian Far East, northern China and possibly North Korea. They have the largest home range of any tiger species because they live in areas with low prey density so they have to search far and wide for food.

The Amur tiger reached the brink of extinction in the 1940s with only about 40 left in the wild. Since then protection and breeding programs have helped the population grow, and it is currently fairly stable at around 540 individuals.

INTERESTING FACT: LIKE HUMAN FINGERPRINTS, NO TWO TIGERS HAVE THE SAME STRIPED PATTERN.

AMUR TIGER

B IS FOR...

| CONSERVATION STATUS: ENDANGERED | POPULATION: 10,000–25,000 |

The blue whale is the largest animal on the planet. Weighing up to 150,000 kilograms, they grow to around 24-30 metres long and have a heart the size of a small car. They are also the loudest animal on earth, with a call louder than a jet engine that can be heard from hundreds of miles away in deep water.

Despite their immense size, blue whales are gentle creatures and have no teeth. They eat over 3000 kilograms of krill every day. Blue whales are found in all oceans except the Arctic.

During the 20th century, the blue whale was pushed to the brink of extinction by commercial whaling. Following a global ban on hunting, blue whale numbers have recovered slightly but they remain endangered. Blue whales face several serious threats including collisions with ships, the overfishing of krill and climate change.

INTERESTING FACT: A BABY BLUE WHALE WEIGHS ABOUT 3500 KILOGRAMS AT BIRTH AND GROWS ABOUT 90 KILOGRAMS A DAY.

BLUE WHALE

C IS FOR...

| CONSERVATION STATUS: VULNERABLE | POPULATION: 5000-6000 |

The crested penguin is a medium-sized species of penguin that lives on rocky Antarctic islands and in the dense rainforest region along New Zealand's Fiordland Coast. They are about 60-68 centimetres tall, and weigh 3-6 kilograms.

Crested penguins spend most of their time in big groups, both on land and at sea, but they usually hunt alone. They are carnivorous, surviving on a diet of mostly squid, krill and small crustaceans.

The natural predators of crested penguins are seals, sharks and killer whales, but they also face significant threats from introduced land species such as cats and foxes, as well as rats and weasels that hunt their eggs. Crested penguins are endangered due to these introduced species in New Zealand as well as deforestation, human disturbances and accidental deaths caused by the fishing industry.

INTERESTING FACT: CRESTED PENGUINS MATE FOR LIFE AND BOTH PARENTS TAKE TURNS TO INCUBATE THE EGGS.

CRESTED PENGUIN

D IS FOR...

| CONSERVATION STATUS: VULNERABLE | POPULATION: AROUND 85,000 |

Dugongs are large, vegetarian marine mammals that are often referred to as sea cows due to their habit of grazing on seagrass meadows.

Dugongs live in tropical and subtropical coastal waters of the Indian and West Pacific oceans, with the majority of the remaining global population in northern Australian waters. Dugongs can live for up to 70 years and grow to 3.5 metres in length, weighing up to 400 kilograms.

These languid and peaceful animals make easy prey for hunters and were once sought after for their meat, oil and teeth. Dugongs are now legally protected but their population is still declining as a result of fishing, hunting, climate change, coastal pollution and the degradation of seagrass meadows.

INTERESTING FACT: DUGONGS SOMETIMES BREATHE BY STANDING ON THEIR TAILS IN SHALLOW WATER.

DUGONG

E is for...

CONSERVATION STATUS: ENDANGERED	POPULATION: AROUND 5000

Eastern gorillas are one of four species of gorilla and the world's largest living primate. The species is divided into two subspecies and they are both endangered – Grauer's gorilla (formerly known as the eastern lowland gorilla) is most populous while the mountain gorilla has only around 700 individuals remaining in the wild.

Eastern gorillas live mostly in the Democratic Republic of Congo and parts of Rwanda and Uganda. They live in large, stable family groups that can number up to 35 individuals, led by a dominant silverback male.

The biggest threat to their survival is habitat loss caused by humans and illegal poaching. Civil unrest in the region has also taken a huge toll on the gorilla population.

INTERESTING FACT: EASTERN GORILLAS IN THE WILD HAVE BEEN SEEN USING BASIC TOOLS TO MORE EFFECTIVELY GATHER FOOD.

EASTERN GORILLA

F IS FOR...

CONSERVATION STATUS: CRITICALLY ENDANGERED	POPULATION: AROUND 13,000

The Fijian iguana is a large, spectacularly coloured lizard that is only found in Fiji. These iguanas grow up to 75 centimetres in length with crest spines up to 1.5 centimetres long.

Of the approximately 13,000 Fijian iguanas that survive, about 12,000 of these exist in one population on a small, single island, making this species extremely vulnerable.

Habitat loss and introduced species are the primary reasons for the decline of this lizard, in particular the introduction of goats to the Fijian islands in a bid to improve quality of life for the human population.

Fijian iguanas eat a very limited variety of native plants, so deforestation for farming purposes has had a huge impact. Alongside the goats, feral cats and introduced species like rats and mongooses also threaten the Fijian iguana's survival.

INTERESTING FACT: THE FIJIAN IGUANA CAN CHANGE COLOUR RAPIDLY FROM GREEN TO BLUE TO BLACK WHEN THREATENED.

FIJIAN IGUANA

G is for...

CONSERVATION STATUS: VULNERABLE	POPULATION: ABOUT 1800

Giant pandas are one of the most well known endangered animals due to their lovable appearance and use in popular culture. Despite their cute appearance, pandas have extremely strong jaws used for crushing bamboo and they can be as dangerous as any other species of bear.

Giant pandas live mainly in bamboo forests high in the mountains of western China. Because bamboo is nutritionally poor, they need to eat up to 20 kilograms of it a day, which takes up most of their time.

Although they were once hunted for their fur, pandas are now considered a national treasure in China. Recent growth in numbers and efforts to protect the species recently resulted in their status being downgraded from endangered to vulnerable. This is encouraging, however they are still threatened by erosion of their habitat due to clearing for agriculture and also the loss of a local variety of bamboo.

INTERESTING FACT: DESPITE THEIR SIZE AND LACONIC NATURE, GIANT PANDAS ARE EXCELLENT TREE CLIMBERS AND GOOD SWIMMERS.

GIANT PANDA

H is for...

CONSERVATION STATUS: CRITICALLY ENDANGERED	POPULATION: UNKNOWN

This very large species of hornbill grows to over one metre tall and is found on the Malay Peninsula and in Indonesia. The current population is unknown but a severe decline is predicted over the next 50 years as hunting pressure and habitat loss are expected to increase.

This spectacular bird is highly prized for its solid horn, called a casque, on top of its beak. This has been illegally traded through organised crime networks for use in carved decorations, like ivory, or for use in traditional medicine.

Helmeted hornbills generally live in areas targeted for logging or palm oil plantations. They have very specific nesting and dietary requirements, so land clearing has a particularly devastating effect.

INTERESTING FACT: HELMETED HORNBILLS HAVE STRANGE CALLS THAT SOUND LIKE 'TOOK, TOOK' FOLLOWED BY MANIACAL LAUGHTER.

HELMETED HORNBILL

I IS FOR...

CONSERVATION STATUS: ENDANGERED	POPULATION: 20,000–25,000

The Indian elephant is one of three subspecies of Asian elephant and is native to mainland Asia, from India and Nepal across to Thailand and Vietnam. Smaller than African elephants, which are also endangered, Indian elephants grow to around 2-3 metres tall and weigh between 2000 and 5000 kilograms.

The main threat to Indian elephants is habitat loss and degradation, driven by expanding human populations. Elephants like feeding on crops such as bananas, rice and sugarcane, leading to conflict with humans. Elephants have also lost much of their territory to hydroelectric projects, palm plantations, highways and other industrial developments.

Poaching for ivory is also a serious threat to Indian elephants, a threat which continues to this day despite efforts to halt the ivory trade.

INTERESTING FACT: ELEPHANTS EAT UP TO 150 KILOGRAMS OF PLANTS A DAY, WHICH CAN TAKE THEM UP TO 19 HOURS TO CONSUME.

INDIAN ELEPHANT

J is for...

CONSERVATION STATUS: ENDANGERED	POPULATION: 250-1000

The jocotoco antpitta, an endangered bird from Ecuador and Peru, was only discovered in 1997. It is unusually large for this type of bird, around the size of a small melon, and it is a mystery how it managed to remain undiscovered for such a long time.

These shy, strange birds have round bodies and long legs that they use like pogo sticks to hop around the forest floor.

Jocotoco antpittas inhabit a very small region of wet, mossy forests in pockets of south Ecuador and northern Peru.

The population of this shy bird is not accurately known, but is presumed to be small due to its tiny range and the declining quality and availability of its habitat.

INTERESTING FACT: THE NAME JOCOTOCO IS ONOMATOPOEIC FOR THE JOCOTOCO'S UNIQUE OWL-LIKE CALL.

JOCOTOCO ANTPITTA

K is for...

CONSERVATION STATUS: CRITICALLY ENDANGERED	POPULATION: 126

The kakapo is one of the largest parrots, growing up to 60 centimetres in height, and is only found in New Zealand. They weigh 2-4 kilograms, making them the heaviest parrot in the world and, as such, the only flightless one.

The nocturnal kakapo is sometimes referred to as the owl parrot because of its large, owl-like head, eyes and call. Their favourite food is the fruit of the rimu tree, but when unavailable, they will eat other seeds, nuts and berries.

The kakapo is thought to have once thrived in New Zealand because there were no natural predators except for humans. The introduction of cats, foxes and weasels by European settlers has resulted in the defenceless kakapo being almost completely wiped out.

INTERESTING FACT: KAKAPOS ARE GOOD CLIMBERS AND ALTHOUGH THEY CAN'T FLY, THEIR WINGS ARE USED LIKE A PARACHUTE WHEN JUMPING OUT OF TREES.

KAKAPO

L IS FOR...

CONSERVATION STATUS: VULNERABLE	POPULATION: AROUND 60,000

The leatherback sea turtle is named for its unique shell, which is leathery rather than hard like the shells of other turtles. They are the largest turtle on earth, growing up to two metres long and weighing over 900 kilograms.

Only one in a thousand turtle babies survive to adulthood, with the females spending around five years at sea before returning to the same beach on which they were born to lay their own eggs.

These ancient creatures have survived for more than a hundred million years, but are now facing extinction. They are listed as vulnerable but many subpopulations are critically endangered.

Although their distribution is wide, numbers of leatherback turtles have seriously declined during the last century as a result of intense egg collection, damage caused by the fishing industry and pollution.

INTERESTING FACT: THE TEMPERATURE INSIDE THE LEATHERBACK TURTLE'S NEST DETERMINES THE SEX OF THE HATCHLINGS.

LEATHERBACK SEA TURTLE

M IS FOR...

CONSERVATION STATUS: VULNERABLE	POPULATION: AROUND 3000

The colourful, curious mandrill is the world's largest monkey. They live mostly in tropical rainforests in the equatorial African countries of Cameroon, Gabon, Equatorial Guinea and the Congo.

Mandrills eat a wide variety of food, mostly fruits and plants but also invertebrates and occasionally vertebrates such as tortoises, rats and even small antelopes.

The mandrills sleep in different trees every night, walk on their toes on all four limbs when on the ground and have been observed in the wild using sticks to clean themselves. The mandrill's peaceful communication can involve silently baring their teeth and shaking their head, while signs of aggression include staring, slapping the ground and bobbing their head.

Deforestation has affected the mandrill, however the main threat to these monkeys is hunting for meat.

INTERESTING FACT: MANDRILLS HAVE POUCHES INSIDE THEIR CHEEKS THAT ARE USED TO STORE SNACKS FOR LATER.

MANDRILL

N IS FOR...

CONSERVATION STATUS: ENDANGERED	POPULATION: AROUND 1500

The numbat, sometimes called the banded anteater, is a small marsupial found only in Australia.

Numbats are rarely seen as their size and appearance enable them to blend into their surroundings, and they dart into cover, usually hollow logs, at any sign of danger. They feed exclusively on termites, needing to eat up to 20,000 a day.

Numbats are the only marsupials that are fully active during the day, when they spend most of their time looking for termites. They have the best vision of all marsupials and, like most ant-eating species, have unusually long tongues.

Numbats are threatened primarily by feral cats and foxes.

INTERESTING FACT: NUMBATS HAVE MORE TEETH THAN ANY OTHER LAND MAMMAL, BUT THEY ARE UNDERDEVELOPED AND NOT USED FOR EATING.

NUMBAT

O IS FOR...

CONSERVATION STATUS: ENDANGERED	POPULATION: AROUND 50,000

Orangutans are the world's largest tree-climbing mammal. They live solitary lives in the forests of Sumatra and Borneo where they feast mostly on tropical fruits like mango, lychees and figs.

There are two types of male orangutan: flanged and unflanged. Flanged males have prominent cheek pads, called flanges, a throat sac used to make loud calls, and a long coat of darker hair on their backs. Unflanged males look like females, although they can reproduce just like flanged males. An unflanged male can change into a flanged male at any time for reasons not yet understood. Orangutans are the only primate in which this odd biological phenomenon occurs.

Orangutan numbers are rapidly declining primarily due to loss of habitat to agricultural use, mostly for palm oil plantations. They are also at threat from illegal logging, forest fires, illegal hunting for meat and the exotic pet trade.

INTERESTING FACT: THE NAME ORANGUTAN MEANS 'PERSON OF THE FOREST' IN THE MALAY LANGUAGE.

ORANGUTAN

P IS FOR...

CONSERVATION STATUS: CRITICALLY ENDANGERED	POPULATION: AROUND 80

The pygmy three-toed sloth is the smallest of all sloth species due to insular dwarfism, which is when a population is confined to an island and must adapt to limited resources.

They have a tiny range, living only on Isla Escudo de Veraguas in the islands of Bocas del Toro, Panama. The island is only 4.3 kilometres square and is around 17 kilometres off the coast.

These sluggish creatures move through the canopy at around 40 metres a day, munching on leaves, buds and twigs. Sloths spend about 15 to 20 hours a day sleeping.

The island is uninhabited but has seasonal visitors such as fishermen, tourists and locals who hunt and harvest wood. Despite the island being protected as a wildlife habitat, the growing tourism industry is contributing to habitat degradation.

INTERESTING FACT: SLOTHS COME TO THE FOREST FLOOR ONLY ONCE A WEEK TO RELIEVE THEMSELVES.

PYGMY THREE-TOED SLOTH

Q is for...

CONSERVATION STATUS: VULNERABLE	POPULATION: 7000–17,000

The quokka is one of the smallest species of wallaby. It is only found in a few tiny areas of Western Australia, both on the mainland and on Rottnest Island and Bald Island.

Quokkas seem to prefer areas that have been burned in the last ten years. They are browsing herbivores who eat a variety of plants but show particular preference for new young growth. Quokkas are also good tree climbers and often do so to reach food.

Mainland quokkas are under considerably more threat than those on the islands due to the impact of introduced foxes and feral cats as well as deforestation and the destruction of habitat caused primarily by feral pigs.

INTERESTING FACT: THE TREND OF TAKING SELFIES WITH THE UNAFRAID AND SEEMINGLY SMILING QUOKKA HAS LED TO THEM BEING CALLED THE HAPPIEST ANIMAL IN THE WORLD.

QUOKKA

R IS FOR...

CONSERVATION STATUS: VULNERABLE	POPULATION: LESS THAN 10,000

The red panda is an acrobatic animal that lives mostly in the trees in high altitude forests spanning Nepal, northern Myanmar and central China.

Red pandas grow to around the size of a domestic cat, although their big, bushy tails add almost half a metre to their size. They are shy and solitary creatures that forage at night and sleep in trees during the day.

The name panda is said to come from the Nepali word 'ponya', meaning bamboo or plant eating animal, which is fitting as pandas are primarily herbivores.

Red pandas are endangered due the destruction of their habitat as more and more forests are destroyed by logging and expanding agriculture.

INTERESTING FACT: RED PANDAS USE THEIR BIG, BUSHY TAILS LIKE A WRAP-AROUND BLANKET TO KEEP WARM IN WINTER.

RED PANDA

S IS FOR...

CONSERVATION STATUS: ENDANGERED	POPULATION: 1000–7000

The rare and magnificent snow leopard lives high in the mountains of Central Asia. Its powerful build allows it to easily scale steep slopes and it can leap six times the length of its body.

Snow leopards have thick fur to keep them warm. Their long tail is used for balance but also wraps around them when resting for warmth. They have wide, fur-covered feet that act as natural snowshoes, helping to distribute their weight over soft snow while also protecting their soles from the cold.

Snow leopards prey mainly on wild sheep and mountain ibex as well as smaller creatures such as hares and game birds. Snow leopards seem to have developed a taste for domestic animals, which has led to many leopards being killed by humans in retribution.

Snow leopards also suffer from habitat loss, the decline of the snow leopard's preferred large mammal prey, and poaching for their pelts.

INTERESTING FACT: UNLIKE OTHER BIG CATS, THE SNOW LEOPARD CANNOT ROAR.

SNOW LEOPARD

T IS FOR...

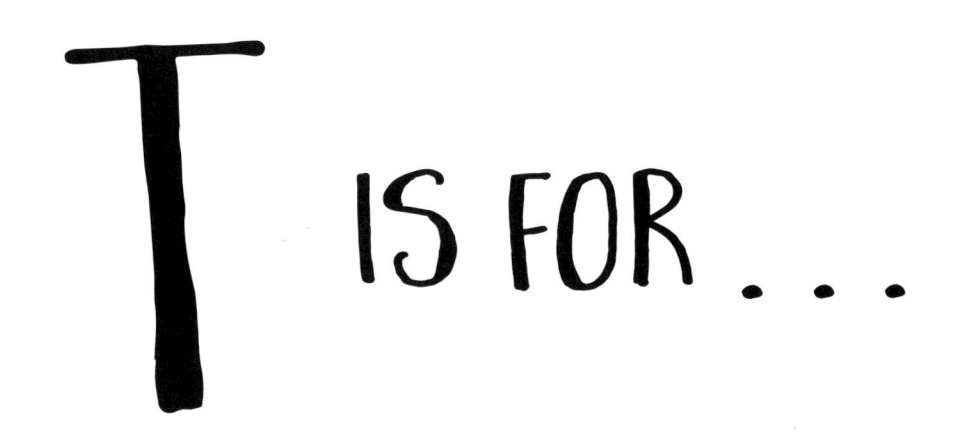

CONSERVATION STATUS: ENDANGERED	POPULATION: 10,000–25,000

The Tasmanian devil is the world's largest carnivorous marsupial. Despite its small size, the devil can sound and look very fierce with its unique, spine-chilling screech and reputed bad temper that led to European settlers naming it the devil.

Devils are limited to the island of Tasmania now, but it is believed they once roamed the mainland of Australia before the introduction of the dingo. They are nocturnal scavengers with powerful jaws that allow them to eat their prey completely – bones, fur and all.

Famous for rowdy communal feeding habits, devils use various noises and displays to establish dominance within the pack.

This Tasmanian icon wasn't always so revered, with trapping and poisoning almost driving the devil to extinction prior to their protection in 1941. Devil numbers recovered, even thrived, for many years until the discovery of the Devil Facial Tumour Disease in the 1990s. This fatal, infectious and so far incurable disease has wiped out much of the population.

INTERESTING FACT: THE DEVIL'S FAMOUS GAPE IS MORE FROM FEAR AND UNCERTAINTY THAN FROM AGGRESSION.

TASMANIAN DEVIL

U is for...

| CONSERVATION STATUS: ENDANGERED | POPULATION: 10,000-20,000 |

The umbrellabird is found in the rainforests of Central and South America. Umbrellabirds are ecologically important as they spread seeds from the fruit they eat.

There are three species of umbrellabird and all are threatened: the bare-necked umbrellabird, the Amazonian umbrellabird and the wattle-throated umbrellabird.

The main threat facing the umbrellabird is habitat loss. Mining, logging and the conversion of rainforest to agricultural areas have caused considerable destruction to the rainforests where umbrellabirds live.

Hunting is a lesser but still significant threat to their survival as umbrellabirds are captured to be sold as exotic caged birds.

INTERESTING FACT: MALE UMBRELLABIRDS PERFORM COURTSHIP DISPLAYS FOR FEMALES TO WATCH BEFORE CHOOSING A PARTNER.

UMBRELLABIRD

V IS FOR...

| CONSERVATION STATUS: CRITICALLY ENDANGERED | POPULATION: ABOUT 60 |

The vaquita is the most endangered marine mammal in the world. They are only found in the northern part of Mexico's Gulf of California, mostly in groups of 2 to 4, although groups of up to 10 have been reported.

Vaquitas are also the world's smallest marine mammal, measuring up to 1.5 metres in length. They are inconspicuous and elusive creatures with a strong aversion to boats. Rather than jumping, vaquitas rise to breathe with a slow rolling movement that barely disrupts the surface of the ocean.

This little porpoise wasn't discovered until 1958 and just over half a century later they are on the brink of extinction. The main threat to vaquitas is being trapped in gillnets by illegal fishing practices. They also suffer from the effects of pollution, habitat degradation, commercial fishing and poaching.

INTERESTING FACT: THE NAME VAQUITA MEANS 'LITTLE COW' IN SPANISH.

VAQUITA

W IS FOR . . .

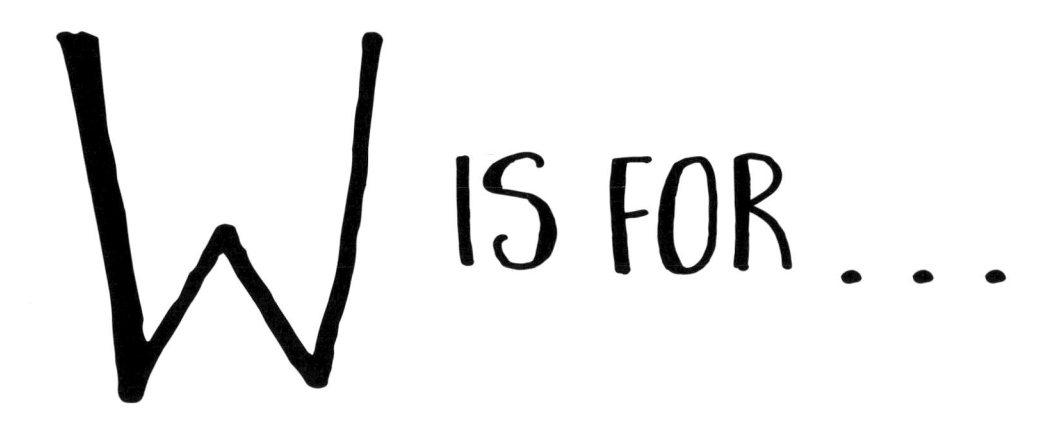

CONSERVATION STATUS: ENDANGERED	POPULATION: AROUND 7000

The whale shark is the world's biggest fish, reaching up to 10 metres long. They have huge mouths up to 1.5 metres wide that contain over 300 rows of tiny teeth. Whale sharks are filter feeders that mostly eat plankton and are docile creatures that are no threat to humans or other larger mammals.

These solitary, gentle giants roam all the oceans of the world but show a distinct preference for warm waters. They migrate to the continental shelf near the west coast of Australia once a year.

The main threats to whale sharks are hunting and tourism. Despite their protected status, they are still illegally hunted for their meat, fins and oil. Whale shark tourism can also be destructive as it interrupts their natural feeding patterns and sharks can be easily injured by boat propellers.

INTERESTING FACT: LIKE HUMAN FINGERPRINTS, EVERY WHALE SHARK HAS A UNIQUE PATTERN OF SPOTS.

WHALE SHARK

X IS FOR...

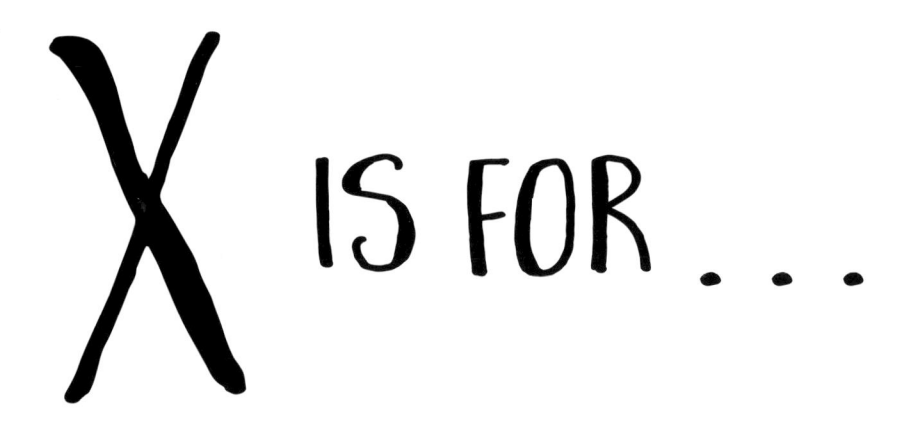

CONSERVATION STATUS: NEAR THREATENED	POPULATION: AROUND 10,000

The Xinjiang ground jay, also known as Biddulph's ground jay, is a small bird endemic to China. They are mostly found in the scrublands of the Taklimakan Desert in the Xinjiang region of western China.

This little bird is considered near threatened due to its small, fragmented population size. Numbers are declining due to habitat destruction caused by intensive grazing of goats and camels, logging for fuel and conversion of large areas to irrigated land.

The Xinjiang ground jay is also threatened by the dramatic increase in human population in the region. It is very likely the conservation status of this bird will soon be upgraded to vulnerable or endangered.

INTERESTING FACT: THE XINJIANG GROUND JAY'S BOWL-SHAPED NEST IS MADE OF TWIGS AND IS PLACED LOW IN A BUSH.

XINJIANG GROUND JAY

Y IS FOR...

CONSERVATION STATUS: ENDANGERED	POPULATION: 1500-3000

Yellow cardinals are large, beautiful, brightly coloured birds found in small pockets of South America.

The yellow cardinal mostly forages on the ground for seeds and grains, but also eats insects and fruit.

Yellow cardinals have a very loud and melodic call that, combined with their striking appearance, makes them a prized song bird.

Chronic exploitation of the species for the pet bird trade is the main reason for their endangered status. Additionally, habitat loss and fragmentation is affecting the survival of the yellow cardinal.

INTERESTING FACT: THE YELLOW CARDINAL HAS A SWEET SONG THAT COMES IN A SERIES OF FOUR TO FIVE WHISTLES.

YELLOW CARDINAL

Z IS FOR...

CONSERVATION STATUS: VULNERABLE	POPULATION: AROUND 10,000

The zebra duiker is a very small antelope and is sometimes referred to as the banded duiker or the striped-back duiker. They live in various parts of West Africa in the dense vegetation of rainforests.

Less than a metre long, these tiny antelopes are herbivores that eat leaves, buds, grass and fruit, as well as droppings from other animals. Both male and female duikers have horns that they use to defend their territory, although zebra duikers are very shy animals that usually hide when they sense danger.

Zebra duikers are considered the least adaptable of duiker species, therefore the most at risk from habitat loss. They are also under threat as they are hunted for both meat and sport.

INTERESTING FACT: BABY ZEBRA DUIKERS ARE BLUEISH IN COLOUR, ONLY RESEMBLING THE COLOUR OF THEIR PARENTS AFTER 7 TO 9 MONTHS.

ZEBRA DUIKER

MORE INFORMATION

I have referred to many websites while writing this book and would encourage you to explore these wonderful sites to find out more:

The World Wildlife Fund: www.worldwildlife.org

Arkive: www.arkive.org

Australian Wildlife Conservancy: www.australianwildlife.org

The International Union for the Conservation of Nature (IUCN) is the world's main authority on the conservation status of species. I have used classifications from the IUCN Red List to describe the conservation status of each animal. The Red List classifies animals into nine categories using criteria such as population size, habitat range and rate of decline. The categories are:

Extinct: No known individuals remaining.

Extinct in the wild: Known only to survive in captivity, or as a naturalised population outside its historic range.

Critically endangered: Extremely high risk of extinction in the wild.

Endangered: High risk of extinction in the wild.

Vulnerable: High risk of endangerment in the wild.

Near threatened: Likely to become endangered in the near future.

Least concern: Lowest risk. Does not qualify for a more at-risk category.

Data deficient: Not enough data to assess its risk of extinction.

Not evaluated: Has not yet been evaluated against the criteria.

For more information go to www.iucnredlist.org

ACKNOWLEDGEMENTS

Most of all, I would like to give my utmost thanks and appreciation to the individual humans and the organisations large and small that spend their time working with and for the protection of the amazing creatures I have drawn for this book.

Huge thanks also to my mum, Gail, for her invaluable help researching and proofreading this book, and my dad, Phil, for his unfailing belief in me.

Many thanks to my team at Red Parka – Katie, Jocelyn, Skye and Greta – who keep everything afloat when I'm lost in kakapo feathers or mandrill hair for days on end. You guys are the best and I feel truly blessed to have such good people around me.

And finally, to my partner, Tracy, for the endless love, support, encouragement and cups of tea (then coffee, then tea again, then coffee again). Every day with you is magic.

ABOUT THE AUTHOR

Jennifer Cossins is a Tasmanian artist and writer with a passion for nature, the animal kingdom and all things bright and colourful.

A born and bred Tasmanian, Jennifer also designs homewares, textiles and stationery, which she stocks in her store, Red Parka, in Hobart, Tasmania.

Jennifer's other books include *The Baby Animal Book* and *101 Collective Nouns*.

REDPARKA.COM.AU